WRITE OUTSIDE

OUTDOOR ACTIVITIES AND WRITING PROMPTS FOR ENGLISH COMPOSITION

Amy Lynn Hess

Gypsy Daughter

Write Outside:

Outdoor Activities and Writing Prompts for English Composition

Print Edition:

ISBN: 978-0-9718068-8-7

Gypsy Daughter

gypsydaughter.wixsite.com/amylynnhess

Contents

Preface

Thank you for purchasing this text to use to help improve your writing skills. Whether for use as a required text in English composition or as a supplemental text for its outdoor activities and writing prompts, I hope the book meets your needs. I also hope you are as excited to try the activities and writing prompts as I am to share them with you and my own students.

I've searched for several years for ways to link outdoor activities to the basics of effective writing. As one of the best ways to clear our minds and think deeply about our own ideas, being outdoors is intrinsically linked to these basics. Being outdoors is not only about "unplugging" or taking a break from technology, but also offers students innumerable opportunities to experience a tangible, natural world. The psychological and physiological benefits of sunshine and fresh air cannot be underestimated. Additionally, structured or group-based outdoor activities give students shared, meaningful experiences on which to base their writing. Structured outdoor activities can help students who otherwise do not have an opportunity develop an appreciation for the natural world. The greatest gift simply being outdoors offers is the gift of quiet moments for unbroken thought. What is writing if not the culmination of hours of unbroken thought?

I have divided the book's contents into three sections based on three core concepts of English composition: *Modes of Communication*, *Rhetorical Appeals*, and *The Writing Process*. Each section has been further divided into chapters that can be completed in any order, or the chapters can be used as supplemental readings, assignments, or bridging exercises in coordination with other texts. Key words and phrases that may be unfamiliar to students have been indexed.

The outdoor activities suggested in each chapter are based on the idea that active learning practices are an inclusive pedagogy. These practices help students engage with one another, reduce their fears of writing, and increase successful completion of composition courses. The activities are appropriate for most geographical locations at any time of year, and for those working alone or with others. The activities give students opportunities to draw upon their creativity, practice both divergent and critical thinking skills, and collaborate. The activities might culminate in discussions, finished art projects, musical compositions, notes for use in written drafts, group projects, or multimedia presentations.

The writing prompts are also broad and can be adapted by faculty in a variety of ways, including assignment length, scope or word count, level of formality, research requirements, and formatting or citation style. The instructions for each writing prompt also leave room for student creativity and individuality. Each chapter's instructions follow the steps in the writing process, which are briefly explained within the instructions and explained in greater detail in the third section of the book. Drafts that stem from the writing prompts might emerge as prewriting exercises, journal entries, graded written assignments, research documents, outlines, speeches, group presentations, blog posts, online discussions, or submissions to publishers.

To put it succinctly, the outdoor activities and guided writing prompts are meant to be useful in whatever ways faculty and students may need them to be – all while giving them permission to simply spend time outdoors.

Amy Lynn Hess

August 11, 2020

Introduction: Paragraphs and Essays

Writing Prompts: Writing Paragraphs and Essays

The writing prompts in each of the following chapters can be completed by writing either a stand-alone paragraph or a short, multi-paragraph essay. Whether writing one paragraph or a longer essay, students should attempt to follow the steps in the writing process as outlined in each prompt. More information about each step in the writing process appears in the third section of the text, *The Writing Process*.

Writing Paragraphs

A paragraph is a collection of sentences grouped together to support one single topic and idea about that topic. Sometimes that topic is the only topic a writer wants to explore, and sometimes that topic is part of a larger whole, like in an essay. Writers divide essays into paragraphs in order to make distinctions between one sub-topic or main idea and another. Each paragraph is set apart not only by shifts in the topic and main idea, but by the use of formatting, like indentations or line spacing.

Structure of a Paragraph

A paragraph can either begin or end with a topic sentence, which controls the content of the paragraph by indicating the paragraph's main idea. Every sentence in a paragraph relates in some way to the main idea stated in the topic sentence. Writer's show that relationship between sentences by using transitional words and phrases that help readers transition from one idea to another.

A body paragraph within an essay includes a topic sentence and evidence in support of that topic sentence. Well-written body paragraphs also contain transitional words and phrases that create logical transitions between and among ideas.

Stand-alone paragraphs, or independent paragraphs, are structured like "mini-essays." An independent paragraph will have a very short introduction that leads into the topic sentence, a topic sentence, evidence relevant to the topic sentence, transitions between and among ideas, and a brief conclusion. The structure of an independent paragraph is indicated by its outline, which writers complete during the organization stage of the writing process.

Example Outline for an Independent Paragraph

- **Lead-in (rhetorical question and startling facts):** Have you ever wanted to try drawing with a pen, but you didn't because you didn't *have* a pen? Well before the invention of the pen as we know it today, ancient Egyptians used reeds, the Spanish used feather quills, and various people around the world used brushes and sticks to draw and write with ink.
- **Topic sentence:** <u>Creating your own pen is as easy as trimming and shaping sticks you gather outdoors.</u>
- **Evidence with transitions:** First, gather a variety of sticks and twigs that are roughly the shape and size of

an average pen. Next, clean and smooth them with sandpaper or steel wool. Lastly, use a sharp knife or file to shape the tips. You can create flat tips, split tips, or pointy tips in a variety of sizes, depending on your preferences. Use store-bought ink or create your own from natural materials in order to create your drawings.

- **Conclusion:** Whether you use your homemade pens once or for years, you will gain a sense of accomplishment just from creating them.

Writing Essays

An essay is a writer's opportunity to discuss a nonfiction topic or idea with a reader in more depth than a paragraph will allow. On the other hand, unlike a research paper, an essay stems from a writer's own experiences and interests, knowledge, and educated opinions. Although essays often contain some source content as evidence, essays contain less source content than a formal research paper.

Although an essay can consist of only one paragraph, an essay is most often a collection of paragraphs grouped together to support a topic that's been divided into sub-topics. Each sub-topic is explained in its own body paragraph with its own topic sentence and evidence relevant to that topic sentence.

Structure of an Essay

Just as a topic sentence indicates the main idea of a paragraph, a thesis statement indicates the main idea of an essay. The thesis statement includes both the topic of the essay and the writer's tone, which is their attitude toward or opinion about the topic. Some thesis statements include a summary of the essay's subtopics, depending on the complexity of the writer's ideas.

Essays are divided into three main sections: the introduction, the body, and the conclusion.

Introduction

The introduction of an essay serves several purposes. First, it attracts the attention of the intended audience, sometimes directly referring to the intended audience by name or description, like when a writer states, "If you are an avid mountain climber, you may be interested in knowing the ins and outs of avoiding a fall."

The introduction is also a good place for writers to introduce any relevant credentials or experience: "Having been an outdoor recreation professor for the past thirty years, I know that even experienced climbers occasionally fall."

A third purpose is to introduce the thesis statement, both topic and tone, in one or more sentences. "Mountain climbers, both experienced and novice, should always be prepared for a fall. They should carry a first-aid kit and a reliable form of emergency communication." It's worth noting, however, that in some types of essays the thesis statement is included in the conclusion instead of the introduction.

Lead-in techniques that help capture the audience's attention, establish a tone, and prepare a reader to accept a claim include narratives, shocking or thought-provoking statements, and familiar quotations and allusions.

- Narratives that illustrate an applicable incident or event are effective lead-in techniques, whether a brief bit of dialogue or an extended anecdote. Storytelling is an ancient method for making meaningful connections.
- Shocking or thought-provoking statements can capture a reader's attention immediately. They are most effective when they are carefully constructed as relevant to the thesis. The statements might be based on facts and statistics, but they might also address a misconception or common misunderstanding. A writer might also use a paradoxical statement or pose a carefully constructed rhetorical question.
- Familiar quotations or allusions can also capture an intended audience's attention because they bring with them an abundance of cultural connotations that make it easy to establish a tone. For example, a writer might describe a landmark or place well-known to the intended audience, or they might choose to capture their attention with popular or meaningful song lyrics.

Body

The body of an essay includes the body paragraphs. Each body paragraph is comprised of one topic sentences and evidence in support of that topic sentence. To continue the example from above, one body paragraph would be about carrying a first aid kit, and a second would be about carrying a reliable form of emergency communication. Because body paragraphs are part of a larger essay, they do not have their own introductions and conclusions.

Conclusion

Writers use the conclusion of an essay to leave readers with a strong impression of the writer's ideas. Although conclusions do not have topic sentences, the most basic conclusion may reiterate the thesis statement and main ideas of an essay. There are other techniques, however, which include offering a broader view of the topic, making the topic applicable to the readers' lives, using narratives or description as a visceral or sensory experience, using humor or wordplay, or inviting a call to action.

The structure of an essay is planned on an outline during the organization stage of the writing process.

Example Outline for an Essay

- **Introduction:**
  - o **Lead-in (narrative that uses emotional appeal and establishes credibility):** My climbing partner for twenty-five years was airlifted by an emergency team after four hour wedged between two boulders. We were able to find her quickly because she was carrying an emergency radio, and we were able to bandage her cuts because we had a properly stocked first-aid kit. Having been an outdoor recreation professor and mountain climber for over thirty years, I can attest that accidents happen, even to experienced climbing teams.
  - o **Thesis Statement:** The best advice I can give any climbing team, novice or experienced, is to prepare for the occasional fall by carrying a well-stocked

first aid kit and a reliable form of emergency communication.

- **Main Idea One**: First aid kit
- **Main Idea Two**: Emergency communication

- **Body Paragraph One**:
  - **Topic Sentence:** <u>Every mountain climber should carry a first aid kit for their own safety and the safety of their partners.</u>
  - **Hypothetical Example:** In addition to including the basics, a climber's first aid kit should include additional items related to the most common mountain climbing accidents and injuries, like abrasions and pulled muscles or tendons.
  - **Real Examples:** That may include ice packs, antibiotic creams, or even splints and wraps.

- **Body Paragraph Two:**
  - **Topic Sentence:** <u>Every climber should also carry a reliable form of emergency communication.</u>
    - **Hypothetical Example:** Sometimes that's as straightforward as carrying a mobile phone, but in some areas there may not be coverage. In those instances a walkie-talkie or radio may be more prudent.
    - **Real Examples:** There are also low-tech options, like whistles and reflective surfaces. A mirror or reflective emergency blanket for signaling rescue teams, should it become necessity, can be extremely useful.

- **Conclusion:** The difference between life and death for a climber who's fallen might be the difference between carrying a first aid kit and communication device or leaving home without them.

Modes of Communication

When writers begin contemplating a new work, they begin by thinking about the work's audience, focus, and purpose. The three of these elements together help a writer determine the best mode of communication for their work.

Writing for an Intended Audience

The intended audience is the person or group of people with whom the writer intends to communicate. Writers should have an intended audience in mind before they begin writing so they can make decisions about their work that will best benefit that particular audience. When writers consider their audience, they think about what makes that reader or group of readers unique because writers want to meet those readers' unique needs. Writers think about what those readers already know or need to know about a topic in order to choose evidence that's the most likely to interest and benefit them.

For example, examples are a great way to explain information to an audience who is unfamiliar with a topic, but examples can become tedious when the audience is already knowledgeable and is seeking additional, specialized information. On the other hand, readers may simply want to be entertained. A letter to a friend or family member is not the right place to explain geometric proofs; however, that friend or family member may want to read a funny story about the writer's college experience.

Once writers determine their intended audience for a particular piece of writing, they carefully use language and evidence relevant to that audience throughout their work.

Writing with Focus

After choosing a topic, and while considering the audience, writers also think about how to narrow a broad topic, like "a funny college experience," into a more narrowed topic, like "falling into the retention pond during a biology class field trip." Another example might be "ants" as a broad topic, and a specific type of ant habitat as a narrowed and more focused topic. Writers who focus their work by narrowing their topics can offer readers more in-depth and interesting information.

Writers control the focus of an essay with its thesis statement, and writers control the focus of a paragraph with its topic sentence. The evidence that appears in a paragraph, whether it's part of the body of a longer essay or a stand-alone paragraph, must be relevant to the statement of the main idea.

The thesis statement or topic sentence does not only indicate the main idea or the topic and tone the writer has chosen, but it also prepares the reader for the type of essay or paragraph they'll be reading. For example, "By the time I crawled out of the pond, I learned that wearing the right shoes on a field trip is more important than I originally thought" prepares the reader for a story. "The most interesting ant habitat is created by the *Dinoponera* ants" does not sound like the beginning of a story, however. Instead, this sentence prepares readers to learn something new about *Dinoponera* ant habitats.

Writing with a Purpose

While thinking about their intended audience and specific focus, writers also contemplate their purpose for writing, and that purpose is directly linked to what's called a mode of communication.

The four modes of communication are description, narration, exposition, and persuasion. The type of persuasion most often required of college writers is called argumentation. Although in a final draft a writer may have used attributes of more than one mode, the finished work will have one distinguishable purpose.

Description

Medical professionals and police officers often use description, or the descriptive mode, in the workplace when they write medical notes and incident reports. The purpose of the descriptive mode is to use specific, concrete and sensory details in order to convey information and support a dominant impression. That dominant impression becomes the main idea, whether that's a thesis statement in an essay or a topic sentence in a paragraph. A dominant impression in the medical profession might be that a person is ill with a particular condition, for instance. Descriptive details help support that impression.

Narration

The purpose of narration is to tell a true story that helps a reader learn a life lesson or experience a moment of insight along with the narrator. The writer uses a chronological organization to tell parts of an experience that lead the reader to a statement insight. That moment of insight or revelation becomes the thesis statement or topic sentence. Sometimes that insight is the punchline of a joke or funny story, like learning about muffler maintenance, and sometimes it's a serious revelation, like the meaning of life.

Exposition

Exposition is the mode writers choose when they want to explain or inform. Encyclopedias, textbooks, dictionaries, and other reference texts are purely expository. Thesis statements and topic sentences in exposition are based on the topic and the writer's tone or attitude toward the topic, like why understanding the topic is helpful, important, or beneficial to the intended audience. Organizational strategies that help writers organize expository paragraphs and essays include comparison and contrast, cause and effect, division and classification, process analysis, illustration or example, and definition.

Persuasion and Argumentation

The purpose of persuasion is to convince or persuade an intended audience to do something or believe something. The type of persuasion that relies on reason and evidence to convince or to persuade is called argumentation. The thesis statement or topic sentence in argumentation is a succinct, declarative statement of the writer's claim or position on the topic. A thesis that also includes a statement of the writer's reasoning is called an enthymeme. For example, "The migratory patterns of birds is important for gardeners to understand," is a thesis statement. "Knowing the migratory patterns of birds can help gardeners protect their produce" is an enthymeme because it also includes the reason why the writer is making the claim of "importance."

Reminding your roommate to eat a healthy salad for dinner is a form of persuasion. You may say to your roommate, "Eat a salad for dinner instead of pizza." This brief suggestion may or may not persuade your roommate. Argumentation using reasons and evidence might be more convincing. In order to use the argumentative mode you might say, "Eat a salad for dinner instead of pizza because we're supposed to go camping tonight, and you'll want to feel well. The last time you ate pizza you had a stomachache and had to go to bed early." This line of reasoning and supporting evidence may not convince a different intended audience, but it is probably the best type of evidence to use to convince your roommate to eat a salad.

Although each mode of communication has its own characteristics, and most writing is a combination of two or more of the modes, the writer's goal remains the same no matter the mode: to communicate as effectively as possible with an intended audience. The main difference among the modes is the way in which the writer's message is organized and presented.

Description and the Descriptive Mode

Although each mode of communication relies on description as a type of evidence to add interest and create a unique experience for readers, the descriptive mode relies the most heavily on descriptive evidence. The most effective descriptions use specific language and concrete words instead of abstract language or adjectives and adverbs. The smell of a rotten egg is a concrete image, for example, because a reader can visualize and smell it. However, "spicy" is an abstract adjective. Although readers may be able to imagine what the writer means by "spicy," the reader's idea of "spicy" may be very different from the writer's idea of it. To make the idea more specific, a writer might replace "spicy" with the name of the spice, like paprika, jalapeno, ginger, or cayenne pepper.

Description is often organized spatially, meaning a writer describes a scene from left to right, inside to outside, background to foreground, top to bottom, or in any way a human (or camera) might encounter an event, object, person, or place. In order to make details flow logically from one to another, writers include transitional words and phrases that indicate the direction of movement through a scene. In addition to using a spatial organization, writers might also use a categorical organization for description, listing the senses by category: sight, sound, smell, taste, texture, and sometimes even the "sixth sense," gut instinct or intuition.

Because there is often so much to describe, writers choose details based on the thesis statement or main idea for the description, which is a broad statement of the writer's dominant impression of the subject.

For example, if a writer's dominant impression of their college roommate is that she is funny, the writer might include a description of the way she laughs and makes faces when she tells jokes, her hilarious Halloween costume, or the way others laugh and smile when they're around her. The writer would not include her annoying habit of leaving dirty dishes in the bathroom sink because it doesn't fit the dominant impression. Furthermore, if focusing on her hilarious Halloween costume, the writer could describe it from top to bottom, starting with her hat, moving down to her false teeth, and subsequently describing each piece of the costume down to her huge shoes. Alternatively, the writer could describe it based on what caught their attention first, which might be the smell of hairspray, followed by a visual description of all the glitter and glue used to make her dress.

Outdoor Activity – Creating an Outdoor Space

"Each place is the right place--the place where I now am can be a sacred space." – Ravi Ravindra

Spend time outdoors creating a comfortable, usable space, then deconstruct that space and "leave no trace." Create a space that works best for you and your circumstances, whether that's pitching a tent, setting up a temporary bench, or sitting on a picnic blanket. Work alone or with others.

Take notes about your sensory experiences while creating, using, and deconstructing your space. If you'd like, divide your notes into six columns, one each for sights, sounds, smells, textures, tastes, and gut instincts or intuitions. Write concrete words in each column as appropriate and based on your observations. For example, you may list "traffic" as a smell or a sound, and you may list "dust" as a texture or a taste, depending on your experience. You may have a "gut instinct" or sense of accomplishment when you leave your space as you found it. If you've worked with others, compare your notes when you've finished.

Writing Prompt – Senses: Describing an Outdoor Space

Summary: Write a sensory description of the temporary space you created, used, and deconstructed.

Goal: Use a dominant impression as your main idea, and support it with concrete, specific language.

Steps:

- **Prewriting:** Complete the outdoor activity and notes. Choose an intended audience, a specific reader or group of readers for whom you are writing. Look over your notes and choose a dominant impression and the sensory experiences that support that dominant impression.

- **Organization:** The mode for this prompt is description, so choose an organizational strategy relevant to the intended audience and dominant impression. For this assignment, either a spatial organization or a categorical organization, categorizing details into each of the senses, is appropriate. These strategies will work for your description no matter its length. For a more formal organization, create a key-word or topical outline.

- **Drafting:** Draft an introduction with a thesis statement or topic sentence that concisely captures your audience's attention and indicates your dominant impression. Support the dominant impression with sensory details. Draft topic sentences for body paragraphs if your description is long enough to be divided into paragraphs. Include a brief conclusion that makes your description meaningful or memorable. Make any revisions or edits that are on your mind while drafting, but set your writing aside and take a break before revising.
- **Revision:** Check your writing for unity, coherence, and clarity. To check for unity, check to be sure you've maintained your dominant impression throughout the description. To check for coherence, check to be sure your transitional words and phrases help readers follow your organizational strategy. To ensure clarity, check your grammar, mechanics, and usage. Additionally, check your content to be sure you have used evidence that proves the accuracy of your dominant impression. If possible, complete revision with a partner or in a group.
- **Formatting:** Give your writing a descriptive and unique title that reiterates the subject of your description and the dominant impression. Review any additional course-specific requirements.

Narration and the Narrative Mode

Writers use the narrative mode of communication to convey information by telling a true story in chronological order or using chronological organization, which is the order in which events took place. A narrative paragraph might appear within an essay as a type of evidence, or an entire essay might be written in the narrative mode no matter the essay's length. The purpose of using narration is to use the story to offer wisdom or insight to readers, wisdom or insight that can only be obtained by reading about, and therefore reliving, the experience the writer has had. Much like "the moral of the story," a statement of insight or revelation often ends a narrative essay.

The types of transitional words and phrases used in narration include references to time and place in context of the story. For example, a writer might use "Before the day started," or "As I was entering the building," as transitions between ideas. Other elements of narration include characterization, the use of a first person narrator, figurative language, sensory description, and dialogue.

Many writers employ the narrative frame technique, which is the use of an introduction and conclusion to frame the main events of the narrative. To organize a narrative frame, a writer begins by explaining in the present tense why the story has been on their mind, a link to present day, or something that's happening in the present that has triggered the memory of the experience. In the body of the story, or the middle of the essay, the writer shifts to the past tense as they recount chronological details of an event or events that took place further in the past. A writer ends the narrative in the present tense as they reflect and share a lesson or insight with their readers. This lesson or insight is something they have only been able to realize by looking back at their chosen event or events. Inclusion of that revelation or insightful thesis statement about an authentic experience is what sets a narrative apart from other forms of stories. Familiar narrative forms include biography, autobiography and memoir, general creative nonfiction, and personal essays.

Outdoor Activity – Walking the Path

"If you're walking down the right path and you're willing to keep walking, eventually you'll make progress." — Barack Obama

Spend time walking outdoors. You may choose to walk for as long as you are comfortable in whatever outdoor space you feel safe. Walk alone or with others.

Take notes that describe the sensory experiences of your walk in chronological order, and capture any insightful, humorous, or informative revelations you might have. You can choose to take notes at the end of your walk or if you stop to take breaks. Although you may prefer to ride a bike, rollerblade, or take a skateboard, walking allows more time to focus on the environment and surroundings.

The revelations you have could be as simple as realizing there are a lot of birds in your neighborhood, or as deep as a metaphorical connection to a complicated circumstance in your life. If you choose to walk with others, be sure to share insights with one another.

11

Writing Prompt – Reliving the Walk: Narration and Storytelling

Summary: Write the narrative of your walk.

Goal: Construct a narrative using first person pronouns, a chronological organization with appropriate transitional words and phrases, and an insightful thesis or topic sentence. If you'd like, add a narrative frame, figurative language, sensory descriptions, and dialogue.

Steps:

- **Prewriting:** Complete the outdoor activity and notes. Choose an intended audience, a specific reader or group of readers for whom you are writing. Look over your notes and choose an insight or revelation you'd like to share and the moments from your walk that support that insight or revelation. Keep in mind that the process of narration is the process of reliving an event in such a way that the readers relive it with you. Such is the ancient power of storytelling.

- **Organization:** The mode for this prompt is narration, so the organizational strategy is chronological, with or without a narrative frame. For a more formal organization, create a key-word or topical outline.

- **Drafting:** Draft a thesis statement or topic sentence that concisely indicates your revelation or insight. Add descriptions and chronological narration in the past tense to support the revelation or insight. You may choose to include an introduction in the present tense that explains your "trigger moment," and a conclusion in the present tense that includes your revelation or insight. Make any revisions or edits that are on your mind while drafting, but set your writing aside and take a break before revising.

- **Revision:** Check your writing for unity, coherence, and clarity. To check for unity, check to be sure you've told a story that helps readers accept your revelation or insight. To check for coherence, check to be sure your transitional words and phrases help readers follow your chronological organization, and carefully check verb tenses for consistency. To ensure clarity, check your grammar, mechanics, and usage, and be sure you have used enough evidence to help a reader share in your experience. If possible, complete revision with a partner or in a group.

- **Formatting:** Give your writing a descriptive and unique title that reiterates the thesis or main idea's claim. Try basing your title on your revelation or insight. Review any additional course-specific requirements.

Exposition and the Expository Mode

The purpose of the expository mode of communication is to explain or to inform. Newspaper articles, encyclopedia entries, and textbooks are examples of the expository mode of writing. Just as in description and narration, expository writing varies in length depending on the scope and depth of the topic, the characteristics of the intended audience, and the complexity of the writer's claims.

Popular organizational strategies for exposition include comparison and contrast, classification, division, definition, illustration, and process analysis or demonstrative writing, like "how-to" articles.

- **Compare and Contrast:** Writers use some paragraphs to explain how topics are alike and some to show they are different. Some essays are all comparative, while others are entirely comprised of contrasts, while still others do both. The introduction or thesis must indicate to the reader why it's important to understand the similarities and differences. An appropriate example topic might be helping readers understand the similarities or differences between being a naturalist and being a survivalist.
- **Classification:** Writers categorize unfamiliar topics in order to help readers understand them, like classifying Olympic events as being part of the Summer Games or Winter Games. Again, the writer should indicate to the reader how the classification is important or aids in understanding.
- **Division:** Writers separate complex topics into smaller components to help readers understand them. For

example, a writer could, figuratively, open a hiker's daypack and place each item from the pack on a table and explain each item's purpose and importance. In an essay, the writer would give each item equal importance, most likely discussing each item in an individual paragraph.

- **Definition:** Writers explain abstract concepts using a variety of types of evidence. The dictionary definition of "fear" is inadequate when telling the story of being stalked while walking, whether in a parking deck or on a trail. The definition of "satisfaction" must be explained in-depth when it's being used to describe the feeling of eating a meal that comes entirely from foraging wild edibles or from a garden.
- **Illustration:** Writers explain a concept using examples, both real and hypothetical. Each new paragraph begins a new example. A writer might want to warn readers about mistakes that can ruin a campout. Each type of mistake the writer wants to explain would have its own paragraph that gave an example of what might happen, hypothetically, or even what has happened to the writer or others.
- **Process Analysis:** Writers explain how something happens or how to do something. The order of details in process analysis is important to a reader's understanding because the process itself is often dependent upon steps being followed in a specific order. Process analysis would be appropriate if explaining how to dig a goldfish pond or explaining how a natural goldfish pond becomes an ecosystem.

In exposition, the thesis statement and topic sentences play an important role in organizing the writer's main ideas and evidence. Types of evidence include real and hypothetical examples, testimony from experts or laypersons, personal observations, formal logic, narratives, sensory descriptions, facts, and statistics. Each of the types of evidence can include information the writer already knows or source content, information the writer finds in sources by completing research. Once writers choose which source content to use to support their claims, they may choose to quote it, using the exact words of the source author, or they may choose to summarize it, shortening it significantly by only reiterating key ideas in their own words. Writers might also choose to paraphrase source content, which means putting key ideas in their own words without significantly shortening the original idea. Writers use transitional words and phrases like "According to," to attribute borrowed content to its original source writers. Writers might also indicate attribution to readers by writing the name of an expert who "states" a fact or opinion. Academic writers also use footnotes or citations and bibliographies to let their readers know where each piece of source information in their writing originated.

In addition to transitions that indicate attribution, transitional words and phrases for exposition include words that indicate categorical organization or order of importance, like "Most importantly." Others indicate a type of evidence, like "For example" and "In fact." Lastly, some transitional words and phrases indicate sequential organization, the sequence of steps in a process, like "First," "Next," and "Once you're finished."

Outdoor Activity – Knowing Flora

"Knowing your ABCs in nature, the flora and fauna, the patterns of the landscape and the rhythm of the seasons is as important as learning how to read and write." – René Redzepi

Spend time outdoors photographing, filming, or drawing flora. In lieu of visual evidence, if you prefer, take descriptive notes.

While *fauna* is a term that refers to the animals that live in a particular region during a particular time, *flora* is a term used to describe the plants that live and grow in a particular area during a particular time. Your examples might be as small as a bit of algae, or a large as an ancient, gnarled, Live Oak or Redwood tree. Work with others to create a more thorough collection.

Once you've created a collection, organize your collection by using classification, which means placing your exhibits into categories. You may need to research plant characteristics or scientific classifications in order to organize your collection. Your categories can be based on scientific classifications, or you can use a less formal, yet creative, classification system.

Writers often research their topics, find content from credible and timely sources, and include and attribute summarized, paraphrased, or quoted source content in their own expository writing. If you're working with others, be sure to share researched information freely.

Writing Prompt – Explaining Plant Properties

Summary: Write an explanation of one or more of the plants in your collection.

Goal: Use the classification strategy and a categorical organization, ideas gathered together by category, to explain plant properties and characteristics.

Steps:

- **Prewriting:** Complete the outdoor activity and notes. Choose an intended audience, a specific reader or group of readers for whom you are writing. Look over your notes and determine how you will categorize the characteristics of your plant. Remember that before you can explain, you must know.

- **Organization:** The mode for this prompt is exposition, and the organization is categorical. The broadest claim or main idea becomes the thesis or topic sentence. In longer essays, the divisions of the main ideas inherent in the thesis become topic sentences. For a more formal organization, create a key-word or topical outline.

- **Drafting:** Draft an introduction with thesis statement or topic sentence that concisely captures the attention of your audience and declares your claim about the topic. Draft topic sentences if your writing requires division by paragraphs for readability. Add evidence to support your main idea and organize it by category or paragraph. Summarize and attribute any source content you use in order to demonstrate credibility.

18

Draft a brief conclusion that leaves a strong impression. Make any revisions or edits that are on your mind while drafting, but set your writing aside and take a break before revising.

- **Revision:** Check your writing for unity, coherence, and clarity. To check for unity, check to be sure you've explained one concise main idea. To check for coherence, check to be sure your transitional words and phrases help readers follow your organizational strategy. To ensure clarity, check your grammar, mechanics, and usage. Finally, be sure you have used enough evidence to help a reader understand new information about your topic. If possible, complete revision with a partner or in a group.
- **Formatting:** Give your writing a descriptive and unique title that reiterates the thesis or main idea's topic and claim. Review any additional course-specific requirements.

Argumentation and the Argumentative Mode

Persuasion is the process of convincing or persuading others to do something or believe something. Argumentation is one form of persuasion. Writers use the argumentative mode of communication when their main goal is to convince or persuade their readers to do something or believe something using reason and evidence. Especially important in argumentation, writers must consider how to use credible, relevant, timely, and reliable evidence to convince or persuade their specific, intended audience.

Argumentation can be structured in various ways. Two popular ways are the problem-solution strategy and the viewpoint strategy.

The problem-solution strategy of argumentation is an explanation of a problem followed by a proposed solution. The thesis is usually a declarative statement of the writer's proposed "best" solution to that problem. Topic sentences help categorize evidence or present reasons why the proposed solution is better than other solutions and how it has the potential to solve the problem. Each reason the writer presents is supported by a variety of types of evidence, including source content.

When writers use argumentation to support a viewpoint, the argument is organized as reasons and supporting evidence in favor of a one viewpoint, position, or attitude about the topic. The thesis is a declaration of that viewpoint, and the topic sentences are stated as reasons the writer has taken that position. If the writer has one main reason for taking that position, they may use an enthymeme as a statement of main idea. When writers choose to include an enthymeme, their topic sentences do not offer additional reasons; instead, their topic sentences introduce evidence that supports the reason stated in the enthymeme. Paragraphs in this type of essay are organized by strength, or order of importance, with the strongest or most important reason stated in the last few sentences or the last paragraph before the conclusion.

The types of transitional words and phrases used in argumentation indicate attribution, points, and counterpoints. "For instance," or "On the other hand" or "However," are commonly used when writing in the argumentative mode. Writers using the argumentative mode also use formal logic and both real and hypothetical examples as organizing principles. When a writer organizes evidence using the order of importance, their final paragraph might begin with "Most importantly."

The argumentative mode often requires especially vigorous prewriting. Writers cannot write convincing arguments until they have considered each of the three parts of an argument: the issue, the evidence, and the reasons why they've adopted a position on the issue. Although it sounds simple, argumentation requires a thorough understanding of the issue at hand from various perspectives, an evaluative review of the evidence, and an ability to articulate unbiased reasons for coming to a conclusion about the issue.

One environmental issue important to many students is whether or not to recycle. Prewriting on this topic would include a complete review of evidence from multiple sources and from multiple perspectives; people who write about why communities should recycle and people who write about why communities should not recycle. After reading ten or more of those sources, investigating the credibility of the source authors, checking the timeliness and reliability of their evidence, looking for biases in those sources, and making sure there were no financial gains for a stakeholder linked to the writer's position, a student might conclude that recycling is something their entire community should do. One reason they believe the community should recycle is because, as many of the sources they read explained with ethically-gathered statistical information, the world is running out of finite resources at an exponential rate. The student might finally conclude that recycling can offset the entire community's use of natural resources.

Only after this extensive amount of prewriting should the student draft a thesis or enthymeme for their argument. In this case, the following enthymeme clearly articulates the student's viewpoint: "Our college community should institute a campus-wide recycling program to offset our abundant use of natural resources."

Because argumentation requires discussion of the issue, the reasons, and the evidence, argumentation often takes the form of an essay with multiple paragraphs.

Outdoor Activity – Building a Cairn

"Some beautiful paths can't be discovered without getting lost." – Erol Ozan

Spend time outside collecting a variety of stones or rocks to build a small cairn, or stack of rocks, in an unobtrusive location. Please note that building a cairn in some locations, like in a national park, is prohibited.

You may need to try multiple times in order to get your stack of stones or rocks to remain standing. Although there may be several ways to stack them, one will be the "best" way, the most aesthetically pleasing or the most stable. Work with others or alone. After it's complete, you may want to disassemble your cairn in order to "leave no trace."

Once you've finished your cairn, take notes about your process. Speculate why one attempt was the "best" and others were not. If you've worked with others, share ideas about how you're each defining "best" and how different attempts were or were not the "best." You may also want to jot down your ideas about other ways people can or should "leave no trace."

Writing Prompt – Issues, Reasons, and Evidence: Building Cairns

Summary: Use the argumentative mode to write about cairns.

Goal: Present reasons for your claim about cairns, and support your reasoning with evidence. You can focus on the best way to build a cairn, why they should or should not be built near hiking trails, offer a solution to the problem that poses, or create an argument based on their proper and original use.

Steps:

- **Prewriting:** Complete the outdoor activity and notes. Choose an intended audience, a specific reader or group of readers for whom you are writing. Think about the "best" way to convince or persuade that particular intended audience about the building or use of cairns. Conduct evaluative research as required to come to a complete understanding of the issue at hand before drafting a thesis, enthymeme, or topic sentence.

- **Organization:** The mode for this prompt is argumentation, and the organizational strategy can be either problem-solution or viewpoint, so a thesis or enthymeme will either be your proposed solution or your viewpoint. The topic sentences might be reasons why you claim that specific solution is the "best" or why you have taken that viewpoint. Alternatively, the topic sentences might be based on evidence that supports an enthymeme, a claim that includes a reason. For a more formal organization, create a key-word or topical outline.

- **Drafting:** Draft an introduction that concisely captures the attention of your audience and declares your claim about the topic. Draft topic sentences as required by your organizational strategy. Add evidence to support your main idea and organize it by paragraph. Summarize and attribute any source content you use in order to demonstrate credibility. Draft a brief conclusion that leaves a strong impression. Make any revisions or edits that are on your mind while drafting, but set your writing aside and take a break before revising.

- **Revision:** Check your writing for unity, coherence, and clarity. To check for unity, check to be sure you've supported one solution or viewpoint. To check for coherence, check to be sure your transitional words and phrases help readers follow your organizational strategy. To ensure clarity, check your grammar, mechanics, and usage. Be sure you have used enough evidence to convince or persuade your reader your viewpoint is reasonable or your proposed solution is viable. If possible, complete revision with a partner or in a group.

- **Formatting:** Give your writing a descriptive and unique title that reiterates the thesis or main idea's claim. Review any additional course-specific requirements.

Rhetorical Appeals

Rhetoric is the use of language to convince or persuade others. When a writer effectively uses emotional appeal, logical appeal, and an appeal to credibility to convince or persuade their intended audience, they have demonstrated the rhetorical appeals known as pathos, logos, and ethos.

To elicit emotional reactions and demonstrate pathos, writers purposefully use vivid descriptions and tell meaningful narratives. Writers provide facts and statistics and use formal logic to demonstrate logos. In order to demonstrate ethos, writers emphasize their own expertise, or they attribute source content and state the credentials of their source content authors, like relevant education and degrees, experience, or job titles. They might also include testimony from experts in the form of quoted, summarized, or paraphrased content.

The key to using each of the rhetorical appeals is to understand the intended audience. Details and ideas that convince or persuade some readers may not convince or persuade others.

Intended Audience

We share our world with a variety of plants and animals. We call the animals of a particular time and place *fauna*, and we call the plants of a particular time and place *flora*.

As the readers of this text, you are my intended audience. I have written each chapter in this book with the intention of explaining the basics of English composition to college students. I have anticipated that the majority of my readers are college students enrolled in composition courses. That said, did you already know the meanings of the terms *fauna* and *flora*? If you already knew, you may have been uninterested in rereading that information, or you may have thought, "I already know this." You may have been distracted from the chapter. On the other hand, if you did not already know those terms, your needs, the needs of my intended audience, were met.

To reiterate, an intended audience is the person or group of people to whom writers address their thoughts. This might be as intimate as speaking to only one person, like in a letter, or as general as speaking to a nation, like in a President's address to an entire county. Writers anticipate the needs of their intended audiences and strive to meet those needs. Writers analyze the intended audience's characteristics to see if any of those characteristics have an effect on their understanding of the topic. Those characteristics might include age, experience, job or career path, memberships in various organizations, where the readers live, or where they go to school. The analysis of these characteristics helps writers focus their main ideas, determine the types of evidence that will be the most effective, choose an appropriate level of language, and write with a particular purpose. This also helps ensure writers capture and keep the audience's attention while effectively using pathos, logos, and ethos, the three most common rhetorical appeals.

Outdoor Activity – Knowing Fauna

"Maybe it's animalness that will make the world right again: the wisdom of elephants, the enthusiasm of canines, the grace of snakes, the mildness of anteaters. Perhaps being human needs some diluting." — Carol Emshwiller

Spend time outdoors creating a collection of *fauna*, just as you may have already collected *flora* for the chapter on exposition.

Photograph, film, or draw fauna in your area. Try to capture the likenesses of as many examples of fauna as you can. You might also take descriptive notes instead of or in addition to visual evidence, if you'd like. Work alone or with others to create a collection, then use classification to categorize your specimens, or use division to parse out one specimen's characteristics into component parts and pieces.

Use your categorized or carefully divided notes to come to conclusions about metaphorical or symbolic meanings for a few of your examples of fauna. Some examples of symbolic meanings might include ants for "productivity," a dog playing in the snow for "joy," colorful beetles for "beauty," a spider in her web for "patience," a soaring hawk for "freedom," or a twitchy squirrel for "anxiety."

Ask yourself if any of the examples remind you of yourself or someone else in some way? Might the characteristics of any of these compliment your own? What could you learn from them?

If you've worked with others, be sure to share your notes. Come to a state of knowing your own mind before committing to the writing process.

Writing Prompt –Explaining the Symbolism of Fauna

Summary: Explain the symbolic characteristics of one or more of your collected fauna.

Goal: Remain focused on the needs of one specific reader throughout the writing process.

Steps:

- **Prewriting:** Complete the outdoor activity and notes. Choose an intended audience, a specific reader for whom you are writing. Look over your notes and determine which animal or animals and symbolic characteristics you want to explain. There may be one that reminds you of your intended reader. Just remember that before you can explain, you must come to a state of *knowing*.
- **Organization:** The mode for this prompt is exposition, but you should choose a strategy or organizational pattern that you believe will most interest or benefit your reader: comparison, contrast, classification, process analysis, or a "how-to." The broadest claim

becomes the thesis or topic sentence, and in this case it will be a statement about the animal and the symbolic characteristics you want to explain. In longer essays, the topic introduced in the thesis might be broken into paragraphs with topic sentences. For a more formal organization, create a key-word or topical outline.

- **Drafting:** Draft an introduction and thesis statement or topic sentence that concisely captures the attention of your audience and declares your claim about the topic. Draft topic sentences if your writing requires division into paragraphs for readability. Add evidence to support your main ideas and organize it by category or paragraph. Use a variety of types of evidence, like examples of behaviors, factual information with attribution, testimony from experts or laypersons, sensory descriptions, or personal observations. Draft a brief conclusion that leaves a strong impression. Make any revisions or edits that are on your mind while drafting, but set your writing aside and take a break before revising.

- **Revision:** Check your writing for unity, coherence, and clarity. To check for unity, check to be sure you've explained one concise main idea to one specific reader throughout. To check for coherence, check to be sure your transitional words and phrases help that reader follow your organizational strategy. To ensure clarity, check your grammar, mechanics, and usage. Be sure you have used enough evidence to help your reader understand your symbolic representations. If possible, complete revision with a partner, in a group, or even with your intended reader.

- **Formatting:** Give your writing a descriptive and unique title that reiterates the thesis or main idea's claim. Review any additional course-specific requirements.

Pathos

Pathos is an appeal to readers' emotions. When writers use pathos, they use language in such a way as to elicit an emotional response that can help convince or persuade readers to accept their claims about a topic.

When used appropriately, pathos helps capture and keep an audience's attention. In the descriptive and narrative modes, there are several opportunities for writers to incorporate pathos, either in the telling of the story or in the mood created by using words that have connotative meanings, or emotional associations. In expository writing, pathos is most often found in introductions and conclusions: Writers may attempt to capture an audience's attention or leave a strong impression with a startling statistic or a meaningful anecdote. Although it is sometimes used in the persuasive mode, especially in sales and advertising, pathos is not likely to be found in scholarly argumentation, which relies on reason and evidence.

It's important for writers to understand the intended audience before attempting to elicit an emotional reaction. For instance, the following are brief examples of pathos that will appeal only to the emotions of types of readers.

- **Confidence:** *Buying this newly-designed mountain bike will make you the most popular and enviable rider on the trail.*
- **Fear:** *Clean up the riverbank this Saturday or risk losing fishing and kayaking access to it forever.*
- **Pity:** *The foundation for sick manatees desperately needs your donations, and if you don't help the manatees survive, no one will.*

- **Guilt:** *Your outdoor pets won't be around forever, so you better spend time with them while you can. Think about how they feel when you ignore them all day.*
- **Hope:** *Imagine a world with clean water, clean air, and abundant resources for all living things to share. It's possible.*

When used too often, poorly, dishonestly, or when readers would prefer to read verifiable facts and empirical evidence, the use of pathos can have unintended effects. Poorly used ethos might bore or distract readers, causing them to lose interest or ignore a writer's claims. Even worse, poorly used pathos can cause readers to become hostile to a viewpoint instead of adopting that viewpoint.

Appealing to an audience's emotions, in other words, can be exceptionally effective or extremely detrimental to a writer's purpose. Pathos should be implemented carefully.

Activity – Mapping "Home"

"I've always been fascinated by maps and cartography. A map tells you where you've been, where you are, and where you're going — in a sense it's three tenses in one."—Peter Greenaway

Spend time outside observing and creating a map of your "home," which is often encompasses more than your "house." Observe the boundaries, which may be natural or manmade, or both. Include a legend or key, scale, and cardinal directions. Do not refer to any official maps, but create your map based solely on your observations and experiences. You may wish to work alone or with others if you share a similar "home," but your map should be your own.

Once you've finished, compare your map to an official map or to maps made by others. Although your maps may have similarities, make notes about any significant differences.

Writing Prompt – "Mapping" Home

Summary: Write about "home," which can be a complicated and emotional topic depending on personal experiences.

Goal: Use pathos to elicit an emotional response in an intended audience while writing about "home."

Steps:

- **Prewriting:** Complete the outdoor activity and notes. Choose an intended audience, a specific reader or group of readers for whom you are writing. Ask yourself whom you want to address as you share your ideas about "home." Look over your notes and determine a narrowed focus and deliberate purpose that will attract your specific readers.
- **Organization:** Choose a mode and accompanying organizational strategy. Whereas description and narration will offer several opportunities for incorporating pathos, writers using exposition or argumentation generally include pathos only in the introduction to pique readers' interest or in the conclusion to leave a strong impression or make a call to action. Choose the mode that will best meet the needs of your readers. The broadest claim becomes

the thesis or topic sentence, and in this case it will be your narrowed statement about "home." In longer essays, the divisions of the main idea become topic sentences. For a more formal organization, create a key-word or topical outline.

- **Drafting:** Draft an introduction and thesis statement or topic sentence that concisely captures the attention of your audience and declares your claim about the topic. Draft topic sentences if your writing requires division by paragraphs for readability. Add evidence to support your main idea and organize it by category or paragraph. Use a variety of types of evidence as appropriate for the mode and organizational strategy you've chosen. Feel free to include details from your mapmaking activity. Draft a brief conclusion that leaves a strong impression. Make any revisions or edits that are on your mind while drafting, but set your writing aside and take a break before revising.

- **Revision:** Check your writing for unity, coherence, and clarity. To check for unity, be sure you've explained one concise main idea to one specific reader throughout. To check for coherence, be sure your transitional words and phrases help your readers follow your organizational strategy. To ensure clarity, check your grammar, mechanics, and usage. Check your content to be sure you have used enough evidence to support your claim about "home," no matter which mode you've chosen to use. If possible, complete revision with a partner or in a group.

- **Formatting:** Give your writing a descriptive and unique title based on the topic and claim. Review any additional course-specific requirements.

Logos

Logos is an appeal to readers' sense of logic. In order to demonstrate logos, writers often use formal logic, empirical evidence, verifiable facts, testimony from experts, and credible statistics as evidence in support of their claims. Incorporating logos by using expert evidence is an excellent strategy for writing.

However, there is more to logos than using the most credible evidence available. Logos requires that evidence is true as well as valid, meaning presented in a logical order. One way to check reasoning for both truth and validity is to render an argument or claim in the form of a syllogism.

Syllogisms consist of three lines of reasoning: a major premise, a minor premise, and a conclusion. Just like there are mathematical formulas for calculating numerical data, there are formulas for creating syllogisms. When a syllogism uses true statements and a logical order, the syllogism is said to be "sound." When a writer fails to follow one of the established formulas, or the syllogism contains untrue statements, the syllogism is said to be "unsound."

One formula for syllogisms is called the affirming syllogism or a modus ponens. The formula is as follows:

- **If A, then B.** *If today is Tuesday, I have to go to campus to teach class at 6:00 p.m.*
- **A is true.** *Today is Tuesday.*
- **Therefore, B is true.** *Therefore, I have to go to campus to teach class at 6:00 p.m.*

There may be extenuating circumstances that invalidate the conclusion, like whether or not it's a holiday, but in general the syllogism is both true and valid, presented in its established, formulaic order.

The following three sentences make up another type of syllogism called a modus tollens. This syllogism is valid, but it doesn't use specific language; therefore, the conclusion in the third line of reasoning cannot be accepted as true.

- **If A, then B.** *If Rachel were a good sister, she would give me $376.00 for my hiking boots.*
- **Not B.** *Rachel won't give me $376.00 for my hiking boots.*
- **Therefore, not A.** *Therefore, Rachel isn't a good sister.*

In order to demonstrate logos, this line of reasoning requires additional explanation and a more careful use of language. "Good sister" is a more complicated concept than someone who gives a sibling money. "Good" is an example of vague language. The writer has not used a word that specifies a reasonable and universal meaning.

Here is another syllogism that requires correction. The term "really great construction worker" is another use of vague language, and even more concerning, the writer has not presented ideas in a logical order.

- **If A, then B.** *If Ben built the treehouse already, then he's a really great construction worker.*
- **The invalid "B is true" has been used. The valid form of the syllogism *should read* "A is true."** *Ben is a really great construction worker.*

- **The invalid "Therefore, A is true" has been used. The valid form of the syllogism should read "B is true."** *Therefore, Ben built the treehouse already.*

First, the writer must make corrections to the language. If the writer replaces "really great" with "dedicated" or "efficient," the idea of building quickly makes more logical sense. Additionally, the quality of the treehouse needs to be clarified because efficiency and quality are related, not equivalent.

Furthermore, the idea that Ben is an able construction worker does not prove that he's already built the treehouse. The reverse might be true. The writer must amend the order of ideas to make more logical sense.

- **If A, then B.** *If Ben built a sturdy treehouse already, he's a dedicated, able, and efficient construction worker.*
- **A is true.** *Ben built a sturdy treehouse already.*
- **Therefore, B is true.** *Therefore, Ben is a dedicated, able, and efficient construction worker.*

A writer must use diction, syntax, and organizational strategies deliberately and carefully in order to appeal to a reader's sense of logic. Writers can expand lines of reasoning in a syllogism to include evidence of various types to create well-ordered and convincing paragraphs and essays. The extent to which the writer includes true and valid evidence is the extent to which the writer demonstrates logos.

Outdoor Activity – Creating Rhythm

"Where I come from we say that rhythm is the soul of life, because the whole universe revolves around rhythm, and when we get out of rhythm, that's when we get into trouble." – Babatunde Olatunji

Spend time outside listening to natural and manmade rhythms, patterns that help us establish order amid chaos. Choose a rhythm you enjoy and commit it to memory by practicing the rhythm. You can create an instrument using objects you find outdoors, or you can use a percussive instrument you already own. Create phrases, sentences, or other bits of language that mimic your rhythm and help you remember it. If working with others, separate for a time. Come back together later to share and practice your rhythms with each other. There's power in rhythms, both simple and complex.

While fresh in your mind, make notes about your rhythm, your phrasings, and your practice session. Find ways to represent your rhythm as accurately as possible on the page.

Writing Prompt – Expository Writing: Teaching Rhythm

Summary: Write instructions for counting and playing your rhythm.

Goal: Demonstrate logos by incorporating true and valid (well-ordered) evidence into your rhythmic instructions.

Steps:

- **Prewriting:** Complete the outdoor activity and notes. Choose an intended audience, a specific reader or group of readers for whom you are writing. Look over your notes and determine the best way to represent your rhythm to your intended audience. This may require preliminary research about various systems of rhythmic counting, or you may wish to use the phrases, sentences, or other bits of language you created during your outdoor activity.

- **Organization:** The mode for this prompt is exposition, and the organizational strategy is a directional process analysis in sequential order. This means you give directions in step-by-step order to help them learn how to do something. The broadest claim becomes the thesis or topic sentence, and in process analysis that claim is often a general statement about why the audience should learn the process the writer is teaching. That reasoning might be enhanced by the use of attributed facts or statistics, demonstrating logos. In longer essays, and if the steps in the process can be grouped categorically, those groupings become the subjects of topic sentences. For a more formal organization, create a key-word or topical outline.

- **Drafting:** Draft an introduction and thesis statement or topic sentence that concisely captures the attention of your audience and declares your claim about the topic. Draft topic sentences if your writing requires division by paragraphs for readability. Add evidence to support your main idea and organize it into sequential steps or groupings of steps. Include information about your chosen system of counting as necessary. Summarize and attribute any source content you use in order to demonstrate credibility. Draft a brief conclusion that leaves a strong impression. Make any revisions or edits that are on your mind while drafting, but set your writing aside and take a break before revising.

- **Revision:** Check your writing for unity, coherence, and clarity. To check for unity, check to be sure you've explained one concise main idea. To check for coherence, check to be sure your transitional words and phrases help readers follow your organizational strategy, a series of sequential steps. To ensure clarity, check your grammar, mechanics, and usage. Make sure you have used enough evidence to help a reader understand and replicate each step in your process. If possible, complete revision with a partner or in a group.
- **Formatting:** Give your writing a descriptive and unique title that reiterates the thesis or main idea's claim. Review any additional course-specific requirements.

Ethos

Ethos is an appeal to readers' sense of authority and credibility. When experts write about a topic, they indicate that credibility to their readers in some way. For example, publishers often include short biographical statements alongside published studies, articles, and essays that explain the writer's credentials.

When writers do not have expertise or experience, they build support for their claims using quoted, summarized, and paraphrased source material written by others who do have expertise and experience.

When writers use content from experts, it is essential they not only cite it, but that they attribute that content in context in order to demonstrate ethos. To put it another way, writers should brag about the credibility of their sources, even if just a little bit. For example, instead of simply including a parenthetical citation with source content, writers should take the opportunity to introduce the credibility of the source author by briefly listing the writer's credentials, experience, or title.

Attribution may be as simple as offering the title of a book an author has written before offering readers a quotation from that book:

> *According to Eliot Coleman, author of* The New Organic Grower: A Master's Manual of Tools and Techniques for the Home and Market Gardener*: "The only truly dependable production technologies are those that are sustainable over the long term. By that very definition, they must avoid erosion,*

pollution, environmental degradation, and resource waste. Any rational food-production system will emphasize the well-being of the soil-air-water biosphere, the creatures which inhabit it, and the human beings who depend upon it."

Writers can also give more general information about a source author before summarizing an idea, like referring to an expert as an expert:

Christine Stevens is a well-known expert in sound therapy.

Because it takes time to accumulate experience in a field, many writers build upon the credibility of others and give credit where credit is due, demonstrating an appeal to ethos.

Outdoor Activity – Planning and Planting

"Our most important job as vegetable gardeners is to feed and sustain soil life, often called the soil food web, beginning with the microbes. If we do this, our plants will thrive, we'll grow nutritious, healthy food, and our soil conditions will get better each year. This is what is meant by the adage 'Feed the soil not the plants.'" – Jane Shellenberger, *Organic Gardener's Companion: Growing Vegetables in the West*

The chapter on descriptive writing includes an activity that asks you to create a *temporary* outdoor space. This chapter's activity gives you an opportunity to plan something more *permanent*, to metaphorically (or literally) prepare the foundation for something that will take time and energy before yielding results. Just as in agriculture, you will plan from the ground up and create a fertile place for you to plant *ideas*.

You may want to plan a garden, a courtyard, a small playscape, or even a multi-acre public park. Feel free to sit outside and daydream. The sky is the limit. You might also begin with a gesture, like repotting one plant to start a patio container garden. You can be artistic, and draw or paint a layout or vista. You can get sweaty while tilling a field, or you can master a bit of engineering by building an outdoor pizza oven.

If working with others, share your ideas, notes, and accomplishments throughout the process. Take time to appreciate any personal experiences or expertise each person may have. You may all wish to contribute to one another's plans.

Writing Prompt – Argumentative Writing: Fertile Foundations

Summary: Justify your plans for a permanent outdoor space, like a garden, courtyard, playscape, or public park.

Goal: Demonstrate ethos by including and attributing information from credible sources that supports your ideas.

Steps:

- **Prewriting:** Complete the outdoor activity and notes. Choose an intended audience, a specific reader or group of readers for whom you are writing. Think about the "best" way to justify your plan, preparation, or planting choices to your intended audience. For example, you may pretend you are presenting ideas for a multi-acre park to your city planning commission, or you may be presenting your idea for a raised bed with tomato plants to a roommate or spouse. You may wish to complete preliminary research and evaluate your sources to be sure they are written by experts.

- **Organization:** The mode for this prompt is argumentation, and the organizational strategy can be either problem-solution or viewpoint. The thesis will either be your proposed solution to a problem, perhaps how to "best" prepare your planning area, or your viewpoint, perhaps that a few containers of flowers are the "best" garden for newbies. The topic sentences will be reasons for your claim, or the topic sentences will be based on evidence that supports an enthymeme. For a more formal organization, create a key-word or topical outline.

- **Drafting:** Draft an introduction and thesis statement that concisely captures the attention of your audience and declares your claim about the topic. Draft topic sentences as required by your organizational strategy. Add evidence to support your main idea and organize it by paragraph. Summarize and attribute any source content you use in order to demonstrate credibility. Draft a brief conclusion that leaves a strong impression. Make any revisions or edits that are on your mind while drafting, but set your writing aside and take a break before revising.

- **Revision:** Check your writing for unity, coherence, and clarity. To check for unity, check to be sure you've supported one solution or viewpoint. To check for coherence, be sure your transitional words and phrases help readers follow your organizational strategy. To ensure clarity, check your grammar, mechanics, and usage. Check your content to be sure you have used enough credible and authoritative evidence to convince or persuade your reader that your viewpoint is reasonable or your proposed solution is viable. If possible, complete revision with a partner or in a group.

- **Formatting:** Give your writing a descriptive and unique title that reiterates the thesis or main idea's claim. Review any additional course-specific requirements.

The Writing Process

The main stages or steps of the writing process are prewriting, organizing or outlining, drafting, and revising. Sometimes writers also plan time for research and time to format their finished drafts for submission or publication. Within each of these main stages or steps are several sub-steps or mini-stages. For example, prewriting also includes choosing and narrowing a topic, creating a preliminary thesis statement, dividing the thesis into main ideas, reviewing assignment requirements, and defining a purpose and intended audience. Organizing and outlining includes determining the best types of evidence, planning for order and flow, and logically dividing a preliminary thesis into preliminary topic sentences. In short, a simplified list of the steps would look very similar to the chapter titles in this section of the book. If the steps of the writing process look familiar to you, it may be because they also appear within the instructions for each of the writing prompts throughout the book.

Just remember that although the word "steps" suggests a linear sequence, the steps may overlap or even need repeating. For example, some writers edit and draft concurrently, and others draft and research concurrently. Revising may require additional editing for grammar, mechanics, and usage, but it is mainly a cycle of ensuring a work has unity and focus, coherence and order, and a clarity of ideas. Revising for unity, coherence, and clarity may require drafting additional evidence or even changing the organizational strategy of the entire work. Writers, with practice, find a rhythm with the process and complete each step accordingly.

Each of the following chapters includes additional information about each step and an outdoor activity with writing prompt that focuses on each chapter's designated step in the writing process.

Alternatively, students and faculty may wish to use each chapter to guide the development of papers over a longer period of time. In those instances, students can use each chapter to help guide their completion of that one paper on an alternative topic. Students may wish to begin by working with faculty to design outdoor experiences as a method of prewriting. Although potential topics are too numerous to list in full, the following list of both broad and narrowed topics may be of interest:

- Arts and creativity
  - o Analyzing architectural exteriors
  - o Taking wildlife photographs
  - o Landscaping for curb appeal
- Gardening
  - o Pond maintenance
  - o Growing culinary and healing herbs
  - o Fruit guilds and companion planting
- Animal Husbandry
  - o Coops and enclosures
  - o Fiber production
  - o Raising animals for meat and dairy
- Survival
  - o Building an emergency shelter
  - o Foraging for wild edibles

- o Primitive hunting, fishing or trapping
- Entertainment
  - o Dining al fresco
  - o Building a pizza oven or brick patio grill
  - o Camping or backyard relaxation: stargazing, games, snacks, stories, and songs
- Science
  - o Exploring local anthropological or geological sites
  - o Weather and climate signs
  - o Orienteering or navigating by the stars
- Sports
  - o The best places for paddling, rowing, rafting, boating or sailing
  - o Safe hiking, biking, climbing or mountaineering
  - o Benefits of playing cooperative, outdoor sports

Prewriting and Divergent Thinking

The type of thinking a writer does before beginning a draft is different from the type of thinking called for in later stages of the writing process. Prewriting calls first for divergent thinking, a type of thinking unhindered by preconceived ideas. During prewriting, writers allow themselves to be unhampered by conventional lines of thought. They consider their topics from multiple perspectives before organizing their ideas or beginning a draft.

Writers use clustering, mind mapping, freewriting, brainstorming, looping, listing, discussion, and many other methods of prewriting when starting a writing project. When writers give these types of prewriting techniques their full and undivided energies, they find they can tap into previously unrealized and exciting ideas.

One especially important aspect of all prewriting is for writers to turn off their "internal critics," the parts of themselves that make them question their own abilities or wonder if their ideas are "good enough" or "interesting enough." During prewriting, writers must practice silencing those negative thoughts and nagging doubts. Instead, they must practice allowing themselves to enjoy the freedom of divergent thinking, of finding ideas deep within the recesses of their minds, ideas they didn't even know existed.

Outdoor Activity – Scavenger Hunt

"In every walk with nature one receives far more than he seeks." – John Muir.

Spend time outdoors, with others if possible, creating and completing scavenger hunt lists. Use divergent thinking to create unique and interesting lists, but also think about the needs of your intended audience, your "seekers."

Once finished, discuss and make notes about what you included on your lists, the process of creating the lists, your ability to seek and find, and any aspects of the scavenger hunt that surprised you.

Writing Prompt – Narrative Writing: Preconceived Ideas

Summary: Write a narrative about any aspect of the scavenger hunt that surprised you.

Goal: Tells the story of the scavenger hunt activity. Every detail should help the reader understand the thesis, which will reveal wisdom or insight about a surprising aspect of the activity.

Steps:

- **Prewriting**: Complete the outdoor activity and notes. Choose an intended audience, a specific reader or group of readers for whom you are writing. Look over your notes and choose an insight or revelation about an aspect of the scavenger hunt that surprised you. Surprise is often based on the difference between preconceived ideas and reality, so perhaps explain your preconceived ideas before you retell the events of the scavenger hunt.

- **Organization:** The mode for this prompt is narration, so the organizational strategy is chronological, with or without a narrative frame. For a more formal organization, create a key-word or topical outline.
- **Drafting:** Draft a thesis statement or topic sentence that concisely indicates your revelation or insight. Add descriptions and chronological narration in the past tense as evidence to support the revelation or insight. You may choose to include an introduction in the present tense that explains your "trigger moment," and a conclusion in the present tense that includes your revelation or insight. Make any revisions or edits that are on your mind while drafting, but set your writing aside and take a break before revising.
- **Revision:** Check your writing for unity, coherence, and clarity. To check for unity, be sure you've told a story that helps readers accept your revelation or insight. To check for coherence, be sure your transitional words and phrases help readers follow your chronological organizational strategy. To ensure clarity, check your grammar, mechanics, and usage and be sure you have used enough evidence to help a reader share in your experience. If possible, complete revision with a partner or in a group.
- **Formatting:** Give your writing a descriptive and unique title. Try basing your title on your revelation or insight. Review any additional course-specific requirements.

Writing Prompt – Prewriting an Alternative Topic

Summary: Generate ideas about an alternative paper topic, either assigned or of your own choosing.

Goal: Use three prewriting methods, mind-mapping, freewriting, and listing, to help determine a purpose, focus, and audience for your topic.

Steps:

- **Mind-Mapping:** Complete a mind map for your chosen or assigned topic. Begin by placing your main idea or topic in the center of a sheet of paper. Divide the topic into smaller idea, drawing out those ideas like spokes on a wheel. Further divide the more narrow ideas. Attempt to fill the page, linking ideas in a daisy chain back to the main idea. Use this as a way to help narrow your focus.

- **Freewriting:** Freewrite about your topic. Begin by making a claim about one of the promising topics from your mind map. This is your private freewriting exercise, so feel free to make it silly or serious, figurative or factual. Attempt to support your claim in a quickly written essay. Free associate, if necessary, to keep writing for a minimum of fifteen minutes. It's important to keep writing, even if you write that you can't think of anything to write. When finished, choose the best sentence from the exercise and begin again with that sentence as your starting point. Reread what you've written and try to determine who you may have had in mind as an audience or who might make an appropriate audience.

- **Listing:** Create lists about your topic. If the topic is controversial, perhaps make lists of reasons why you may be for and against the idea. If the topic is divisible, perhaps make lists of ways to divide the topic, or create lists of examples that may help support the topic. Make a variety of types of lists to help you choose a workable purpose, mode and strategy for your topic.

- **Purpose, Focus, and Audience:** Once you are able to articulate an intended audience, narrowed topic, and chosen mode, you can generate a working thesis and are ready to begin organizing your ideas.

Organization and Critical Thinking

Once writers finish generating divergent ideas about a topic, they can begin choosing the best ideas from their lists, clusters, mind-maps, brainstorming, discussions, notes, or freewriting. That change from *generating* ideas to *choosing* ideas indicates the shift from divergent thinking to critical thinking.

Critical thinking is metacognitive. To think critically, writers think about their own thoughts; why they think or believe as they do, when those thoughts developed, who may have encouraged those thoughts, and what actions, ideas, or beliefs those thoughts have subsequently incited. Writers use critical thinking to carefully consider their ideas and think about how those ideas might develop into meaningful written work. It's at this point writers stop and consider how a line of thought might develop, what might convince an intended audience, or what sort of insight they can offer their readers.

The step in the writing process most related to critical thinking is organization, which naturally follows prewriting. Sub-steps of organization include narrowing down a broad topic to fit the scope of an assignment, the creation of a thesis and topic sentences, hierarchical outlining, and generating or finding the most appropriate types of evidence for each main idea. These critical decisions help determine the final structure of the work, a structure that's carefully planned by creating an outline.

An outline will help the writer plan an introduction with attention-getting material appropriate to the intended audience and purpose. The outline will include a thesis or topic sentence, and main ideas or topic sentences appropriate to the mode and focus. The outline must also include evidence relevant to each topic sentence and a conclusion that satisfactorily ends the work. When writing includes source content, that source content's placement and citations are included on the outline, as well.

Outdoor Activity – Sketching a Favorite Tree

"The greatest oak was once a little nut who held its ground." – Napoleon Hill

Spend time outdoors choosing an aesthetically pleasing tree. Sketch the shape of that tree. It might be symmetrical or non-symmetrical, bursting with color or in need of care. The choice is yours.

When finished, note reasons why that particular tree is aesthetically pleasing to you. If you've worked with others, compare your reasons for choosing the trees you've chosen.

Note that the shape of an outline is indicative to the shape of a tree.

Writing Prompt – Sketching an Outline

Summary: Create an outline that organizes your thoughts about why you've chosen to sketch a particular tree.

Goal: Organize and create a well-designed, hierarchical, key-word outline.

Steps:

- **Prewriting:** Complete the outdoor activity and notes. Choose an intended audience and the most meaningful ideas from your notes.

- **Organization:** Develop your own layout or design for an outline or use a common layout or design. An example of a bulleted outline appears in the introduction of this text. A creative option may be to create a hierarchical structure based on the natural shape of a tree. For example, a tree that has three main branches stemming from its trunk would have three main ideas or topic sentences. This can be representational, a numbered or bulleted list, or arranged and drawn artistically.

- **Drafting:** Draft a thesis statement or main idea that concisely indicates your main claim about your favorite tree. The main claim is the "trunk of your tree." State the reasons for your claim as topic sentences. These reasons are the "main branches of your tree." Add evidence to support the topic sentences using the principles of ethos and logos. These are the smaller "shoots of your tree" Include an introduction to capture your audience's attention and a conclusion that leaves a strong impression. You can consider these the "roots and foliage of your tree."

- **Revision:** Check your key words and phrases for unity, coherence, and clarity. Revise and edit as necessary to make your outline clear, yet concise. Be sure you have used a variety of types of evidence. Add citations and a bibliography as required.

- **Formatting:** Give your outline a descriptive and unique title that reiterates the thesis or main idea's claim. Review any additional course-specific requirements.

Writing Prompt – Outlining an Alternative Topic

Summary: Organize your main ideas and evidence about your assigned or chosen topic.

Goal: Draft a well-designed, hierarchical key-word outline that helps establish unity, coherence and clarity.

Steps:

- **Rhetorical Situation:** Write out the intended audience, purpose, and focus at the top of your outline as a reminder to yourself to stay on task. All three should be based on the prewriting activity you completed in the previous chapter.
- **Framework:** Prepare an outline template that divides your plan into an introduction, body, and conclusion. Use bullets or numbers, or use a creative design to create a hierarchy. An example of a bulleted outline appears in the introduction of this text.
- **Introduction:** Under the introduction, create a line item for your attention-getting material or lead-in. Create a line item in the introduction for the thesis, as well, although you may choose to move it to the conclusion later in the writing process. Under the thesis, state each of your main ideas using key words.
- **Body:** Within the body, create a line item for the first topic sentence, which should be a clear statement

about the first main idea. Create one line item per type of evidence you plan to use to support that topic sentence. If any of the evidence is source evidence, be sure to cite it.

- o Create a new line item for any additional topic sentence, and create lines under each new topic sentence for that topic sentence's type of evidence. There will usually be one topic sentence per each main idea listed under the thesis.
- o Additionally, readers appreciate symmetry in evidence throughout paragraphs: If the first topic sentence is supported by a hypothetical example, a real example, a bit of testimony from an expert, and a personal observation, you may wish to plan the evidence for the second topic sentence using the same types of evidence in the same order.
- **Conclusion:** Plan a conclusion that satisfactorily ends the work.
- **Bibliography:** Create a bibliographic list of sources you plan to use, and be sure to include parenthetical citations or attribution within the line items where any source content appears.

Research and Source Content

Writers sometimes conduct preliminary research about a topic while prewriting. This type of general research helps them understand how a topic can be narrowed down, can be broken into sub-topics, or can be divided into various viewpoints. Preliminary research comes from general reference sources or encyclopedias, offers an overview of a topic, and can sometimes be classified as common knowledge. This type of source content does not often become part of a final draft because it is too general, meant only to help a writer understand a topic more thoroughly.

Writers with prior knowledge of a topic, experts as well as those who've conducted preliminary research, conduct *additional* research while organizing and drafting. The most credible, reliable, and relevant source content gathered during this research becomes evidence within the final draft's body paragraphs and adds credibility and logic, ethos and logos, to a writer's claims.

Evaluating Source Content

Before source content is used in a paper, writers must evaluate that content to be sure it's worthy of inclusion.

Credible

First, writers check source content for credibility, which comes from the expertise of the author or publisher and the credibility of the source content they have chosen to use. In order to check for credibility, writers not only check the credentials of the authors or publication in general, but they also research the credentials of each author or publication listed in the source content's bibliography. Although it seems like a herculean task, credentials of authors and publications or their editors can generally be found within the original publication or within an academic library's database.

Additionally, a general sense of credibility can be garnered by looking at publication types. For example, publications called *magazines* are generally written by professional writers for the general population. Publications called *journals* are written by professionals in the field for other professionals in the field. Although both types of articles are well researched and well written, the credentials of writers published in journals are often more relevant to the topic at hand. Attributing content to a trusted expert on the topic will demonstrate a higher level of ethos than attributing content to a professional writer who writes about a variety of topics. This is not to say magazine articles cannot be used as evidence. Quite the contrary, they often make excellent sources. Writers must simply be aware of what's expected by their intended audiences and deliver content appropriate to those expectations.

Reliable

Second, writers evaluate sources by checking the information's reliability, which is a matter of accuracy, truthfulness, and correctness. Writers check reliability by looking at whether or not other experts agree or disagree with the information. They look at how the author's information was acquired. If the writers use statistics as evidence, writers must find out the sample sizes and look to be sure there were no biased or leading questions. Writers also look at how experiments were conducted and whether or not results were repeatable by others, honoring the scientific method. Timeliness can also affect reliability, so writers look to see how old the source information is and how its publication date might affect its worth. Writers might also check to see if the author, publication, or sponsoring organization had any type of financial stake, called a vested interest, in the viewpoint presented in the source content. For example, a weight loss company that sponsors an experiment or survey about weight loss has a vested interest in the results reflecting favorably on their product. They stand to earn more money. If the conclusions do reflect favorably on their product, resulting in additional sales, their vested interest makes the findings less reliable Researchers may have felt pressured to report favorable findings, for example.

Relevant

Lastly, writers look at relevancy, which means the writer considers whether or not the source content helps them support a connected or related point in their own writing. A source that explains the proper identification of wild edibles of Central America might seem relevant in a paper about wild edibles, but not if the paper is about wild edibles of Eastern Europe. Relevancy should also be considered in terms of the reader, the intended audience. If the intended audience has never heard of wild edibles, perhaps source content that explains the potential dangers of foraging would be more relevant – at least for that particular audience.

Attribution and Citation

The type of content that becomes part of a writer's work is more specialized and focused than what can be found in a general reference source. It's written by experts and requires acknowledgement by attribution and citation if any part of it is used in a final draft.

Writers must be transparent when they use source content. They must attribute the content to its original source. Citations are a specialized form of attribution, and there are several citation styles. Common citation styles used in composition courses are the Modern Language Association (MLA) style, and the American Psychological Association (APA) style. Citations for each source for either of these styles appear in two locations. First, attribution within the sentence or a parenthetical shorthand appears within the text of the paper, wherever the writer has quoted, paraphrased, or summarized content. A complete citation that adheres to the guidelines established by the specific style manuals will appear at the end of the writer's paper in an alphabetical listing, a bibliography. In MLA style that bibliography is called a works cited list. In APA style it is referred to as a references list.

There are several online resources that can help students learn how and when to use both in-text citations and bibliographic citations.

Annotated Bibliography

One way writers collect and organize notes about a topic is within an annotated bibliography, which is simply a list of sources about the narrowed topic that the writer has annotated. To annotate means to take notes. An annotation is a note.

The intended audience for annotated bibliographies is often the writers themselves or a project-based group or team whose members are sharing research. Writers collect sources and take notes on those sources. The notes are recorded in such a way that the information can easily be shared and used in a paper in the future.

The types of notes writers take about sources can vary from project-to-project, but often include notes on credibility, reliability, and relevance.

Annotations often include the following five sections:

- Bibliographic publication information in any appropriate citation style
- The author's or publisher's credentials
- A summary or paraphrase of the source's main ideas
- Notes about the types of evidence included
- Notes about the strength of its rhetorical appeals or its credibility, reliability, and relevance, including timeliness

Outdoor Activity – Wondering and Asking

"I loved being outside. We'd hold lightning bugs in our fingers and pretend they were diamond rings." – Loretta Lynn

Spend time outdoors innocently playing pretend. Try to capture the metaphorical spirit of a child: Dandelions and daisies might become crowns, and a trickle of water might become a raging river. Wonder and ask questions like a child: What kinds of birds do you hear? Why can't birds talk? What kind of flowers and plants do you see? Are they safe to eat? What kinds of clouds are in the sky? Can you touch a cloud?

Play with others if possible. Ask questions of one another.

Share your experiences with one another and create a research plan based on a list of all the questions you've asked. Determine what type of information will help you or other members of the group answer your questions. Find research sources that help satisfy your curiosity.

Writing Prompt – Building an Annotated Bibliography

Summary: List and make notes about sources you find that help answer one or more of your "Wondering and Asking" activity questions.

Goal: Use credible, relevant, reliable sources to create a well-structured annotated bibliography for yourself or research team.

Steps:

- **Prewriting:** Complete the outdoor activity and notes. For this annotated bibliography, you and your group members are your own intended audience. You are collecting information and recording in such a way that you can easily use it in a paper in the future.
- **Organization:** An annotated bibliography is purely expository. Record important information from each source you read and organize it consistently across all of your notes on each source. Be sure to share your

organizational strategy with one another if working with others.

- **Drafting:** Draft your notes. First, record the citation information in any appropriate citation style. Next, investigate and record the author or publisher credentials and level of expertise. In a third section, summarize or paraphrase the main ideas. Lastly, take notes about the main types of evidence the author has used and note the strength of its rhetorical appeals.

- **Revision:** Check your writing for unity, coherence, and clarity. Revise and edit as necessary to make your writing clear, yet concise. Even if each annotated bibliographic source has been annotated by different group members, the document should have unity, coherence, and clarity throughout.

- **Formatting:** Give your annotated bibliography a descriptive and unique title that indicates the narrowed topic you've investigated. Be sure your formatting makes it easy to distinguish between each section and subsection of your annotated bibliography. Review any additional course-specific requirements.

Writing Prompt – Annotated Bibliography for an Alternative Topic

Summary: Work with a librarian to find several sources about your narrowed topic and subtopics.

Goal: Evaluate and annotate each source to be sure you include only credible, relevant, reliable sources in your final draft.

Steps:

- **Prewriting:** Gather any preliminary research you completed during prewriting to help you create a list of search terms. Finish your working outline and check its body paragraphs to assess where additional source content may be required. Work with a librarian to find several sources that include content that may be worthy of your final draft.
- **Organization:** An annotated bibliography is purely expository. Record important information from each source you read and organize it consistently across all of your notes on each source. Be sure to share your organizational strategy with one another if working with others.
- **Drafting:** Draft your notes. First, record the citation information in any appropriate citation style. Next, investigate and record the author or publisher credentials and level of expertise. In a third section, summarize or paraphrase the main ideas. Lastly, take notes about the main types of evidence the author has used and note the strength of its rhetorical appeals.
- **Revision:** Check your writing for unity, coherence, and clarity. Revise and edit as necessary to make your writing clear, yet concise. Even if each annotated bibliographic source has been annotated by different group members, the document should have unity, coherence, and clarity throughout.
- **Formatting:** Give your annotated bibliography a descriptive and unique title that indicates the narrowed topic you've investigated. Be sure your formatting makes it easy to distinguish between each

section and subsection of your annotated bibliography. Review any additional course-specific requirements.

Drafting and Evidence

One of the first rules of writing is to support any claims and reasons for those claims with reliable, relevant, and credible evidence. A writer has to understand the needs, attitudes, and knowledge-level of the intended audience and use evidence that will most effectively inform, persuade, or offer meaningful narratives and descriptions to those readers. Additionally, the writer has to know how and when to use different types of evidence based on the writing situation. The writer should strive to use the "best" evidence available to meet the needs of the specific audience in that specific situation.

Once a writer articulates claims and reasons and carefully considers the audience's characteristics, drafting becomes the process of weaving those original ideas with a variety of types of evidence - and any necessary clarifications of the evidence. Writers indicate shifts between and among ideas using transitional words and phrases. For example, using "On the other hand" or "however" indicates a writer is about to offer a counterpoint. "Therefore" indicates when a writer's thoughts come to a conclusion, and "furthermore" means the writer is about to offer additional information. "According to" tells readers they are about to read testimony.

Types of evidence include real and hypothetical examples, expert and lay testimony, personal observations, facts, statistics, narratives, formal logic, and descriptions. While some evidence comes from sources, some evidence originates with the writer and helps the writer demonstrate credibility, like when stating personal observations or using a personal narrative to illustrate a point. It's the combination of types of evidence that helps a writer both meet the audience's needs and maintain interest.

Activity – Grounding

"Man takes root at his feet, and at best he is no more than a potted plant in his house or carriage till he has established communication with the soil by the loving and magnetic touch of his soles to it." – John Burroughs

Spend time outside grounding or "earthing," which is the process of transferring Earth's electrons into your own body. Read about the process, if necessary, before experiencing the sensation for yourself.

When finished, take some time to take notes about what you've learned and about your personal experience and observations. If you've worked with others, share and discuss your research and experiences with them. Listen to their experiences and research notes, as well.

Writing Prompt – Argumentative Writing: Opinion on Grounding

Summary: Write an argumentative essay about grounding.

Goal: Use a variety of types of evidence, including personal observations and experiences, to support a claim about grounding.

Steps:

- **Prewriting:** Complete the outdoor activity and notes. Choose an intended audience, a specific reader or group of readers for whom you are writing. Think about the "best" way to convince or persuade that particular intended audience to adopt your point of view about grounding. Begin thinking about the types of evidence that might be most convincing for that intended audience: testimony from scientists, lay testimony from multiple people, real and hypothetical examples?

- **Organization:** The mode for this prompt is argumentation, and the organizational strategy can be either problem-solution or viewpoint. The topic sentences might be reasons why you claim grounding is a solution to a particular problem, or why you have made a specific claim about grounding. Alternatively, the topic sentences might be based on evidence that supports an enthymeme, a type of thesis that includes a claim as well as a reason. For example, a sentence that offers one main reason why a person should or should not try grounding would be an enthymeme. Use your prewriting notes and research to create a key-word or topical outline.

- **Drafting:** Draft an introduction and thesis statement that concisely captures the attention of your audience and declares your claim about the topic. Draft topic sentences as required by your organizational strategy. Add evidence to support your main idea and organize it by paragraph. Summarize and attribute any source content you use in order to demonstrate credibility. In this essay emphasize your own experiences and observations and carefully construct transitions between ideas. Use first person pronouns as necessary. Draft a brief conclusion that leaves a strong impression. Make any revisions or edits that are on your mind while drafting, but set your writing aside and take a break before revising.

- **Revision:** Check your writing for unity, coherence, and clarity. To check for unity, check to be sure you've supported one solution or viewpoint. To check for coherence, check to be sure your transitional words and phrases help readers follow your organizational strategy. To ensure clarity, check your grammar, mechanics, and usage and be sure you have used enough evidence to help a reader understand new information about your topic. If possible, complete revision with a partner or in a group.

- **Formatting:** Give your writing a descriptive and unique title that reiterates the thesis or main idea's claim. Review any additional course-specific requirements.

Writing Prompt – Drafting an Alternative Topic

Summary: Complete a rough draft for your chosen or given topic based on the prewriting and organization you've already completed.

Goal: Draft unified, coherent, and clear sentences and paragraphs to establish a meaningful connection with your intended audience.

Steps:

- **Thesis:** First, draft a thesis statement that concisely declares your claim about the topic. This may be identical to the sentence on your outline, but you may wish to edit or revise it before placing it in your rough draft. You may or may not want to include a summary list of your main ideas with your thesis.
- **Body:** Next, work on your body paragraphs. Draft topic sentences as required by the organizational strategy you chose during the prewriting and organization stages of the writing process. Use transitional words and phrases to establish connections among and between your ideas and your evidence. Summarize and attribute any source content you use in order to demonstrate credibility. If you choose to emphasize your own experiences and observations as evidence, use first person pronouns as necessary.
  - As you work on your body paragraphs, remember the following
  - Body paragraphs within a longer work do not have their own introductions and conclusions.
  - You can work on the body paragraphs in any order. You can start with the one the interests you the most to help you get started.
- **Introduction:** Once you've completed drafting the body of the essay, draft a brief lead-in for your introduction. The lead-in should attract the attention of your intended audience and transition smoothly into the thesis. Some common lead-in techniques or ways to begin an introduction include narratives, shocking or

thought-provoking statements, and familiar quotations or allusions.

- **Conclusion:** Draft a conclusion that leaves a strong impression. Techniques include offering a broader view of the topic, making the topic applicable to the readers' lives, using narratives or description as a visceral or sensory experience, using humor or wordplay, or inviting a call to action.

- **Revision:** Make any revisions or edits that are on your mind while drafting, but you do not have to revise and edit as you draft. Find a balance that allows you to continue writing satisfactory sentences and paragraphs while silencing your inner critic. Set your writing aside and take a break before revising.

Revision

Revision is the step in the writing process when writers, working alone and with others, make their work better than its first draft. Sometimes it has to be revised several times before it's "perfect," but the goal of revision is always to make the work better.

Writing is both competitive and cooperative. Writing is competitive in that publishers choose what to publish and what to reject, and readers choose what to read and what to ignore. Writers, however, often work closely with one another as proofreaders, editors, cowriters, researchers, and publishers in order to create work that both readers and publishers will appreciate. More than any other, revision is the step in the writing process that allows writers to experience the transformative power of cooperation.

One way to make revision more manageable for both writers and revision partners is by dividing it into tasks based on the three qualities all writing should exhibit: unity, coherence, and clarity.

Unity

To ensure unity, writers check relevancy between main ideas and evidence. The use of language and evidence throughout a paragraph or essay should also be relevant to one purpose and one intended audience.

Essays should have one main idea articulated in the thesis, and each subsequent point in the essay should support that thesis. Likewise, paragraphs have topic sentences supported by evidence relevant to the paragraph's topic sentence.

Coherence

Coherence is the quality of order and flow. To check for coherence, writers check that the chosen mode and organizational strategy are the most appropriate for the topic. They ensure the work demonstrates a logical progression of ideas based on the chosen organizational strategy, like problem-solution, process analysis, or chronological narrative, using meaningful transitional words and phrases. Other ways writers add coherence is by repeating key words and phrases, by using pronouns, by structuring parallel sentences or using refrains, and by creating well-balanced paragraphs or paragraphs of equal importance.

Clarity

Clarity simply means the writing is as clear as possible, both its language and its ideas. One way writers check for clarity is by proofreading and editing for grammar, mechanics, and usage. In order to ensure clarity of ideas, writers also check that there aren't any questions left unanswered or claims left unsupported. Having revision partners, editors, or proofreaders helps writers find those unanswered questions or unsupported claims.

Activity – Having a Field Day

"I feel like going to class every morning is so humbling. You're always working to improve, and you're always being critiqued on your next performance. It's not about what you've done. There's always room to grow." – Misty Copeland

Spend time outside inventing or playing cooperative or competitive games with others. Work within the boundaries of what you have at hand: a city park, field, yard, jump ropes, roller skates, a swimming pool, experience in choreography, a rubber ball, or even just some eggs and spoons. Strive to improve your performances until you're satisfied with your outcomes.

Take notes about your field day experiences. Specifically, note how having (or not having) partners affected your outcomes. If you did have partners, be sure to explain how you think you affected their outcomes, as well. Record specific examples.

Writing Prompt – Narrative Writing: Outcomes

Summary: Write and revise a brief narrative of your field day activities.

Goal: Use the revision process to make each participant's narrative better by focusing on unity, coherence, and clarity.

Steps:

- **Prewriting:** Complete the outdoor activity and notes. Choose an intended audience, a specific reader or group of readers for whom you are writing. Look over your notes and choose an insight or revelation you'd like to share and the moments from your field day that support that insight or revelation.

- **Organization:** The mode for this prompt is narration, so the organizational strategy is chronological, with or without a narrative frame. For a more formal organization, create a key-word or topical outline.
- **Drafting:** Draft a thesis statement or topic sentence that concisely indicates your revelation or insight. Add descriptions and chronological narration in the past tense as evidence to support the revelation or insight. You may choose to include an introduction in the present tense that explains your "trigger moment," and a conclusion in the present tense that includes your revelation or insight. Make any revisions or edits that are on your mind while drafting, but set your writing aside and take a break before revising.
- **Revision:** Check your writing for unity, coherence, and clarity. To check for unity, check to be sure you've told a story that helps readers accept your revelation or insight. To check for coherence, check to be sure your transitional words and phrases help readers follow your chronological organizational strategy. To ensure clarity, check your grammar, mechanics, and usage and be sure you have used enough evidence to help a reader share in your experience. If possible, complete revision with a partner or in a group. For this particular assignment, you may wish to create a revision checklist or draft a list of specific questions you'd like your partner or group to address. Working with others will improve your outcomes. For example, if you know you have difficulty with sentence fragments and coherence, you may wish to add those specific items to your

checklist so your partners will know to look for them. If you know that in the past your titles have been too vague, you might want to ask, "Is my title descriptive or too vague?" Also pay close attention to what your revision partners are asking you to review in their papers.

- **Formatting:** Give your writing a descriptive and unique title that reiterates the thesis or main idea's claim. Try basing your title on your revelation or insight. Review any additional course-specific requirements.

Writing Prompt – Revising an Alternative Topic

Summary: Revise the rough draft you've prewritten, outlined, and drafted on an alternative topic.

Goal: Use the revision process to make your own and a partner's paper better by focusing on unity, coherence, and clarity.

Steps:

- Check your own writing for unity, coherence, and clarity.
  - o To check for unity, read your paper carefully to be sure you have one purpose, one focus, and have satisfied the needs of one intended audience. Look to make sure each main idea aligns with, or is relevant to, an easily identifiable thesis or enthymeme. Check to see if each section or paragraph meets the purpose or follows your chosen strategy: to tell a story that offers wisdom,

offers a meaningful description, convinces or persuades, or informs. Read each sentence in each paragraph and ensure that each sentence is relevant to that paragraph's main idea or topic sentence. Look carefully at your diction and syntax to be sure each is at an appropriate level for your intended audience's level of comprehension.

o To check for coherence, check to be sure your transitional words and phrases help readers follow your organizational strategy. Make sure your sentences flow from one to the next and that your paragraphs build to a natural conclusion. If you've used formal deductive logic, perhaps in the form of a syllogism, check its form for validity. Also look at your use of repeated key words and phrases, your use of parallel sentence structures, and your use of pronouns as substitutes for those key words and phrases. For added stylistic continuity, look at your sentence lengths and structures. Variety in sentence types can add rhythmic coherence to your writing.

o To ensure clarity, check your grammar, mechanics, and usage. Use standard English to help all readers better understand your ideas. Furthermore, be sure you have used enough evidence to help a reader share in your experience.

• If possible, complete your revision with a partner or in a group.

o You may wish to create a revision checklist or draft a list of specific questions you'd like your partner or group to address. Organize your specific checklist or questions by the same qualities as listed above: unity, coherence, and clarity. You may want to incorporate other concepts covered in this text into your checklist or questions, as well. Those include ethos, logos, and pathos; attribution and citation, and formatting per a set of publication guidelines, like MLA or APA.

Publication and Formatting

Before a writer sends work to its final destination, that work must be formatted according to any given requirements and guidelines. An editor may require a specific font, a publisher may require specific placement of contact information, and a research partner may need your contributions by a specific deadline.

Individual publications and professors also generally have requirements regarding length, topic, and mode for specific submissions and assignments. In addition to expecting writers to adhere to the topics dictated by their mission statement or calls for submissions, a publisher may require a short autobiography, a specific number of sources or an accompanying annotated bibliography or outline. Each specific requirement or a set of submission guidelines are generally available on a publication's Web site. Professors in various disciplines may require a discipline-specific format and citation style, like MLA, APA, the Chicago Manual style, or the style used by the Associated Press (AP). Each of these organizations publish manuals, both print and online, to assist writers who are following each set of guidelines.

Because the final destination of the work is such an important element in the writing situation, writers must pay close attention to these requirements and guidelines. Writers should work diligently to make sure they've met each requirement before submitting the work to an editor, publisher, partner, or professor.

Activity – Wind Chimes Assemblage

"The very winds whispered in soothing accents, and maternal Nature bade me weep no more." – Mary Wollstonecraft Shelley

Spend time outdoors creating and hanging wind chimes. Supplement objects you find with objects you've already collected, like the rocks from your cairn, your impromptu rhythm instrument, or your scavenger hunt findings. You may also need hardware and crafting supplies, like wire, string, dental floss, fishing line, glue, or other adhesives and connectors. The requirements are that the wind chimes must move easily in the wind and make a "chiming" sound.

Once finished, observe your wind chimes. Take notes about your process, your outcome, and your sensory experiences. If you've worked with others, compare and appreciate each other's accomplishment.

Writing Prompt – Requirements and Guidelines: Wind Chimes

Summary: Write a short essay about your wind chimes by following a set of formatting requirements or submission guidelines.

Goal: Use the steps in the writing process to meet all the given requirements of a writing assignment. If requirements have not been given to you, follow the submission guidelines of an appropriate magazine or journal of your choice.

Steps:

- **Prewriting:** Complete the outdoor activity and notes. Choose an intended audience, a specific reader or group of readers for whom you are writing: Your intended audience for this prompt may be an editor or publisher for a particular publication. Look over your notes and choose a main idea, which might be a claim or viewpoint, dominant impression, or insight, depending on your mode or purpose.

- **Organization:** Choose an organizational strategy relevant to the intended audience and main idea. For a more formal organization, create a key-word or topical outline.

- **Drafting:** Draft an introduction with a thesis statement or main idea that concisely captures your audience's attention. Add evidence to support the main idea. Draft topic sentences for each paragraph if you've divided your ideas into paragraphs. Include a brief conclusion that leaves a strong impression. Make any revisions or edits that are on your mind while drafting, but set your writing aside and take a break before revising.

- **Revision:** Check your writing for unity, coherence, and clarity. To check for unity, check to be sure you've maintained your main idea throughout the work. To check for coherence, check to be sure your transitional words and phrases help readers follow your organizational strategy. To ensure clarity, check your grammar, mechanics, and usage and be sure you have used enough evidence to prove the accuracy of your main idea. If possible, complete revision with a partner or in a group.

- **Formatting:** Give your writing a descriptive and unique title that reiterates the thesis or main idea's claim. Try basing your title on both the topic and your claim about the topic. Review any additional course-specific or publication-specific requirements. If you feel confident about the quality and relevancy of your work to a publication's call for submissions, submit it proudly.

Writing Prompt –Formatting and Publishing an Alternative Topic

Summary: Format your revised paper by following a set of specific requirements or submission guidelines.

Goal: Use the steps in the writing process to meet all the given requirements of a writing assignment.

Steps:

- Carefully review the formatting requirements for your longer paper given by your professor. Common requirements include word count, relevancy to a given prompt, source content expectations, and the use of a discipline-specific publication style for formatting and citations.
  - o Check your word count using the tools embedded in your word processing program
  - o Check your thesis statement against any prompt you have been given

- Be sure you've met the expectations for source content and citations
- Use the appropriate publication manual to check your overall formatting and citations
- If requirements have not been given to you, follow the submission guidelines of a magazine or journal of your choice. In addition to meeting the topical requirements given in the mission and vision statements of a publication, common requirements include word count, font choice, spacing, and file type.

Final Thoughts

Completing a project is cause for celebration, and especially so when you are proud of your work. It's also a time for reflection, a time to not only be proud of what's been accomplished, but to commit that accomplishment's lessons to memory.

When writing, as with any endeavor, the goal is to be better at the end of the process than when you began. Not only will you know more about the topics you study, examine, and explain, but you'll know more about writing and about your own strengths and weaknesses. The same is true for each new writing project any writer undertakes.

There are a plethora of resources available, well beyond this book, that can help you continue to become a better writer. As you reflect on your accomplishments after having completed the activities and prompts in this text, you might also realize you want to learn more about the topics you've been exploring, like cartography, local fauna, emergency shelters, or the natural world's natural rhythms. You might also realize you want to continue honing your skills in narration, description, exposition, and argumentation. Applicable in every facet of life, the development of those skills is a worthwhile pursuit. Remember that writing is more than a *knowing*, it is a set of skills that continue to develop throughout our entire lives, alongside our ability to think. Writing is an action, a *doing*. The more we take the time to write, the better writers we become.

Index

Acknowledgements

Many thanks to my friends and colleagues who offered not only encouragement, but constructive criticism and sound advice throughout the writing process: Alex Mack, Amanda Ashour, Amy Munn Parker, Jason Miller, and Lynn Dupree.

About the Author

Amy Lynn Hess is an Atlanta area writer, publisher, and English professor. She holds a B.S. in Theatre and Interpretation from Central Michigan University, an M.A. in Theatre History and Criticism from Ohio University, and an M.F.A. in Creative Writing from Naropa University's Jack Kerouac School of Disembodied Poetics.

Other texts by Hess include *Diagramming Sentences: A Playful Way to Analyze Everyday Language*, and *The College Journal*.

To learn more, readers can enroll in her online Udemy courses or read her blog, *Gypsy Daughter Essays*.

Made in the USA
Columbia, SC
19 August 2021